Razia's Ray of Hope

For the courageous women — especially Razia Jan and Patti Quigley —
who work to heal the world, as well as for the brave and enthusiastic
teachers and girls at the Zabuli Education Center in Afghanistan — E.S.

I dedicate this book to all the courageous girls, women, boys and
men who stand up to adversity and who can make a real and positive
change in the world while remaining true to themselves — S.V.

Acknowledgments
Heartfelt thanks to the team who helped me bring
Razia's story to life — Lisa Lyons, Karen Li, Stacey
Roderick, Suana Verelst and Julia Naimska — I value
each of your talents and your collaborative spirit.
— Elizabeth Suneby

I would like to thank Lisa Lyons and Karen Li for
giving me the opportunity to illustrate this most
interesting and important project. A heartfelt
thank you to Julia Naimska and Stacey Roderick
for all the help and advice along the way. A special
thank you to Liz Suneby, whose story inspired me
to illustrate this beautiful and mysterious country
and its people. And finally a very special thank you
to Razia Jan for her courageous and important work
in Afghanistan. — Suana Verelst

Kids Can Press acknowledges the financial support
of the Government of Ontario, through the Ontario
Media Development Corporation's Ontario Book
Initiative; the Ontario Arts Council; the Canada
Council for the Arts; and the Government of Canada,
through the CBF, for our publishing activity.

Published in Canada by
Kids Can Press Ltd.
25 Dockside Drive
Toronto, ON M5A 0B5

Published in the U.S. by
Kids Can Press Ltd.
2250 Military Road
Tonawanda, NY 14150

www.kidscanpress.com

Edited by Karen Li and Stacey Roderick
Designed by Julia Naimska

Page 30: Photo courtesy of
Karen Wong Photography
(www.karenwong-photo.com)

This book is smyth sewn casebound.
Manufactured in Malaysia, in 4/2013
by Tien Wah Press (Pte) Ltd.

CM 13 0 9 8 7 6 5 4 3 2 1

Library and Archives Canada Cataloguing
in Publication

Suneby, Elizabeth, 1958-
Razia's ray of hope : one girl's dream of an education /
written by Elizabeth Suneby ; illustrated by Suana
Verelst.

(CitizenKid)
ISBN 978-1-55453-816-4

1. Jan, Razia — Juvenile fiction. 2. Girls — Education
— Afghanistan — Juvenile fiction. 3. Girls' schools
— Afghanistan — Juvenile fiction.   4. Afghanistan —
Social conditions — 21st century — Juvenile
fiction.   I. Verelst, Suana II. Title. III. Series:
CitizenKid

PZ7.S9145Ra 2013   j813'.6   C2012-908290-2

Razia's Ray of Hope

One Girl's Dream of an Education

Written by
Elizabeth Suneby

Illustrated by
Suana Verelst

Citizen**Kid**™

A collection of books that inform children about the
world and inspire them to be better global citizens

KIDS CAN PRESS

My cousins and I raced down the road to see what the excitement was about. Men and women were gathering around the empty lot in our village. Any time we played in that lot, I'd found shards of clay tiles and not much else.

This day, ribbons brightened the dry earth. Important-looking adults were laying a large stone on the ground. And women passed out chocolates wrapped in shiny papers.

My little sister, Zara, and I collected as many as we could and stuffed them into our pockets before asking for more.

My grandfather spotted us and walked over. I hung my head, afraid he would scold us for taking more than our share of the candy.

Instead, Baba gi pointed proudly to the large cornerstone. "This is where my school once stood."

I knew Baba gi had gone to school. I loved hearing his stories about learning to read and write and calculate numbers. It sounded so exciting.

"What happened to it?" asked my cousin Hamid.

Baba gi looked at the ground. "It was destroyed by seventeen years of war."

"But what's happening today?" I asked. "The Nowruz celebrations are over."

"They are building a new school ... for girls," said Baba gi.

"A school for girls!" Every night I fell asleep dreaming about going to school like my brothers. "Please, Baba gi, ask Baba and Aziz if I may go. I must go."

That evening, like most evenings, I sat by my brothers Jamil and Karim as they studied by lantern light. They attended the boys' school in the next village.

Baba, my father, worked on our farm with my uncles and cousins. My two eldest brothers, Aziz and Ahmad, worked at the quarry, cutting stones. They never wanted to go to school. Like us girls, they could not read or write.

"Jamil, may I have a piece of paper?" I asked.

"Why do you need paper? You don't have homework. You can't even write," said Karim.

Yes, I *could* write! I had memorized the Dari alphabet, and I could spell my name. But I was afraid to tell my brothers. What if they wouldn't let me sit with them? I kept quiet.

Whenever I found Baba gi alone, I would whisper in his ear, "Have you spoken to Baba and Aziz yet?"

"I will. I will, my dear Razia," Baba gi would say as he patted my head. It was always, "I will."

So I turned to my mother for help. "Bibi, have you seen what they are building on the empty lot? Baba gi says it will be a school for girls."

"Yes, I know," Bibi answered as she hurried me and Zara to join our cousins. They were on their way to the village tandoor to bake naan for dinner.

I took my sister's hand. "Please, Bibi, I want to go to school. Girls from our village are registering. Girls from other villages, too. Sara told me when we played hopscotch yesterday."

Bibi handed us our dough and shooed us out the door. I called back, "I need to learn to read and write, Bibi. I promise to teach you! Please talk to Baba and Aziz!"

"I will. I will," said Bibi. She sounded just like Baba gi.

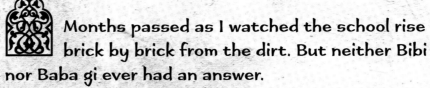 Months passed as I watched the school rise brick by brick from the dirt. But neither Bibi nor Baba gi ever had an answer.

At the beginning of March, the construction crew covered the bricks with white stucco that made the new school shine in the sunlight. They painted the door red, as bright as the flames of the tandoor.

Each morning as I swept the courtyard, I heard girls chatter about the nice woman who started the school and the teachers from Kabul.

Each afternoon as I fetched water from the well, I saw girls on their way home from registration, carrying crisp, new school uniforms over their arms.

One night, as I lay on my mattress, I heard Baba gi call my father, brothers and uncles to a family meeting. I propped myself up to catch every word of their talk.

Baba gi started the jerga. "Razia wants to attend the new girls' school in the village. I support her desire.

"Some of you are too young to remember, and some of you were not even born, but before the occupation of our country, before the civil wars and before the Taliban, women in Afghanistan were educated. They were doctors, government workers and journalists.

"It is time to give our daughters and granddaughters in Deh'Subz the chance to read and write. Our family and our country will be stronger for it."

I couldn't believe my ears. Would I be allowed to go to school?

The jerga continued. It was Uncle Iqbal's turn to speak. "Our girls need to help their mothers at home."

"We need Razia to work in the orchards, too," Uncle Ali added. "Our trees are just coming back after years of drought. And Razia harvests almonds and peaches faster than any of us."

"Razia can complete her chores before and after school. That will be the condition of her enrollment," Baba gi replied.

"Next you'll want Razia to go into town to shop by herself," said my father, wrinkling his forehead.

"Or for women to shed their burqas in public," my brother Ahmad added.

My brother Aziz ended the jerga. "Razia is not going."

Those four simple words made my heart sink.

The next morning, I woke with the sun to practice my reading. From under my pillow, I took out scraps of newspaper that the baker wrapped around our freshly baked naan. Even if I couldn't go to school, I was determined to be the kind of woman Baba gi had described — a woman who helped others through her work inside and outside her home.

After my morning chores, I walked to the school. I passed a stone wall being built around the school grounds, and I knocked on the bright red door. A woman opened it and greeted me with a smile. "Hello, my name is Razia Jan. Come in, please."

I entered a different world. Fresh white hallways, clean classrooms with desks, chalkboards, books, paper and pencils — all in one place! It was unbelievable.

I introduced myself. "My name is Razia, too. I want to come to your school, but my brother and father will not give me permission." I told Razia Jan what I'd overheard at the jerga.

Razia Jan offered to come home with me and speak to Baba gi. Maybe together they could convince the other men to let me attend school.

As soon as Razia Jan and I arrived, I ran off to find Baba gi.

"Baba gi, the maulim shabia from the new girls' school is here to speak to you! Please come greet her. Bring Baba and Bibi." I spoke a mile a minute so as not to waste any time.

Baba gi didn't look surprised to learn I had gone to the school on my own. He and Razia Jan spoke privately for several minutes. Then Baba gi excused himself to find my father and mother.

I stayed out of sight when the three returned to speak to Razia Jan.

Razia Jan thanked my family for their time. Then she described how her school would teach Dari, English, Pashto, math, health and hygiene to younger girls. As the girls got older, the school would teach them how to read the Koran, as well as geography, science, history and algebra.

Razia Jan also explained how her school would provide textbooks, a new uniform and healthy lunches for all students. Best of all, she said, the school would be free.

Baba sounded surprised to hear about
everything the school would provide. He
told Razia Jan he would speak to my brother
Aziz when he returned from the quarry.
But just then, Aziz walked in.

Baba gi spoke up. "Aziz, I did not realize you were home."

Razia Jan turned and introduced herself and her school. She knew Aziz was the one to convince.

"I ask you for your tolerance, if not support, for Razia's education. Please consider, if men are the backbone of Afghanistan, then women are the eyes of our country. Without an education, we will all be blind."

Aziz shook Razia Jan's hand and walked out of the room.

I followed him.

"Agha jan, why are you home so early? Are you feeling sick?" I asked. His face was pale and sweaty.

"Yes, I have a fever. My body aches all over. I stopped for medicine on my way home, but I need Karim or Jamil to read the directions to me. Please get me some water." Aziz closed his eyes.

I poured a glass of water and brought it to Aziz. While he dozed, I picked up the medicine bottle and slowly sounded out the directions.

I looked up and saw Aziz watching me.
"How do you know how to read?" he asked.

"I listen to Jamil and Karim study every
night," I said, counting out his pills according
to the directions. "Please, Agha jan, please
let me go to school. I will be able to help the
family even more if I do."

Aziz took his medicine and smiled. Then
he went back to rest without uttering a word.

Only a couple of days remained before Nowruz and the opening of the girls' school. I sat on the stoop, scrubbing potatoes for the evening's soup.

If I could not attend school, I would ask my friends to share with me what they learned every day. That would be second best, yet far from perfect.

As I picked up the last potato, I heard Aziz approach. "Razia," he said. I peeled the potato quickly to avoid his gaze.

"I have reconsidered. I learned this morning that stones from my quarry are being used to build a wall around the girls' school." Aziz paused. I did not move or make a sound.

"Now I trust that you will be safe in that building, my precious sister. You may attend Razia Jan's school —"

I couldn't contain myself. I leapt up and threw my arms around Aziz. "I promise to stay clear of danger. Thank you, Agha jan."

"But you must complete your household chores before and after classes," Aziz continued.

"I will not let you down, Agha jan. Thank you!"

Soon after, my family celebrated Nowruz in the orchards. We picnicked under the almond blossoms that were the first bloom of spring — and now the sign of a new school year.

On the first day of school, Razia Jan greeted all the students at the gates of the Zabuli Education Center.

"Salam alekum. Welcome." She patted each of us on the back, and we walked through the bright red door of our beautiful new school.

I was led to the third-grade classroom. My teacher introduced herself and then asked each of us to say our name and what we wanted to be when we grew up.

My friend Sara threw her hand up first. "Maulim shabia, my name is Sara, and I want to be an engineer when I grow up."

"What's an engineer?" Marwa blurted out without being called upon.

"I am too young to know that, but when I become one, I will tell you all about it," Sara explained.

Rahila waved her arms, and our teacher picked her next. "I am Rahila, and I want to be a doctor. I will build a clinic in our village and treat all the children for free."

I spoke last. "Maulim shabia, I have always dreamed of being a teacher. And I promised my mother — and my oldest brother, Aziz — that I would practice on them."

Education for Everyone

You might sometimes wish you didn't have to go to school. But can you imagine if you weren't ever *allowed* to go to school? If you never learned how to read or write?

Around the world, about 69 million school-age children are not in school. That's more than the number of people living in the states of Texas and California combined — and more than double the population of Canada!

Almost half of these children (31 million) live in sub-Saharan Africa. More than a quarter (18 million), like Razia, live in Southern Asia. There are many reasons why these children do not go to school, including poverty, political instability, regional conflict and natural disaster. Many children are also kept out of school because their local traditions forbid it. Instead of learning in school, children often must help to support their families, usually by working in jobs that earn very little money.

Razia's story is inspired by the lives of real girls living in the village of Deh'Subz, north of Afghanistan's capital city, Kabul. Only about one-quarter of girls living in developing countries go to school at all. And in Afghanistan, only about 13 percent of women are literate, which means only 13 out of 100 can read and write.

Imagine if your mother couldn't read or write. She wouldn't be able to read you a story, a map or the directions on a medicine bottle. She wouldn't be able to drive a car because she couldn't pass the written test. And there are few well-paying jobs for people who can't read or write, so it's likely your family would not have very much money. By contrast, women who are literate tend to have better incomes, housing and health care. And in turn, they provide these things for their families and communities. Everyone benefits from educating women.

The Real Razia Jan

Razia Jan was born in Afghanistan and moved to the United States when she was a young woman. She worked hard as a tailor and raised her son in a small town in Massachusetts.

After September 11, 2001, Razia felt she needed to connect people from her homeland in Afghanistan and people from her new home in America. In 2007, she started Razia's Ray of Hope Foundation. She hoped to improve the lives of women and children in Afghanistan through education.

In 2008, Razia made the big decision to give up her comfortable life in the United States and move back to Kabul, Afghanistan. She planned to open the Zabuli Education Center for Girls. The education center is in the middle of seven villages that never had a girls' school before.

Today, the center is full of 350 young girls learning to read and write. The students love school so much, says Razia, that they run in the door every day and even beg for school to be all year long, without vacation. Many of the girls take their workbooks home and teach their mothers the lessons! These brave young girls and their commitment to become educated are the inspiration for this book. In recognition of Razia's work, she was honored by CNN as one of their Top 10 Heroes of 2012, an award given to ordinary people doing extraordinary things to make the world a better place.

Razia believes that education is the key to positive, peaceful change in the world. Do you agree?

Razia Jan with students Parwana, Bibi Ayesha and Bibi Begum. The best of friends, the three girls are among the top of their class.

Dari Words

Agha jan: a title of respect

Baba: Father

Baba gi: Grandfather

Bibi: Mother

burqa: the wrap some Muslim women must wear in public to cover themselves fully from head to toe, even their faces

Dari: one of the official languages spoken in Afghanistan, along with Pashto

Deh'Subz: a mountainous village 48 km (30 mi.) outside of Afghanistan's capital city, Kabul. Deh'Subz means "green city" and is named for its vineyards and orchards.

jerga: a decision-making meeting held by the eldest men in the family

maulim shabia: literally, "Miss Teacher"

naan: the traditional flat bread eaten in Afghanistan and many other countries in South and Central Asia

Nowruz: the Persian New Year, which also marks the beginning of spring

Pashto: one of the official languages spoken in Afghanistan, along with Dari

salam alekum: the words for both "hello" and "peace"

Taliban: an extreme militia group that ruled large parts of Afghanistan from 1996 until the Taliban government of Afghanistan was overthrown in 2001. The Taliban does not believe girls should be educated.

tandoor: a clay oven used for cooking and baking foods, including naan

Classroom Activities: A Day in Razia's Life

The activities below are designed to help students
- compare the lives of girls where they live to the lives of girls in Afghanistan
- understand the importance of education and, in particular, educating girls
- consider how they can help kids around the world receive an education

You'll find these activities and much more at CitizenKid Central (**www.citizenkidcentral.com**).

Girls in School

Activity: Have the girls in your class stand up. Ask 60 percent (3 out of 5) of the girls to sit down. Explain that they are not lucky enough to attend primary school in Afghanistan. Of the remaining 40 percent still standing, ask 80 percent (4 out of 5) of those girls to sit. Explain that these girls are not able to finish their schooling. The girls left standing are approximately the number of girls who are actually able to complete a primary-school education in Afghanistan.

QUESTIONS FOR DISCUSSION:
- How many girls in your class expect to finish (primary, middle, high) school?
- How does it make you feel that many girls in Afghanistan and other countries are not able to attend school?
- How do you think these girls' lives will be different from the lives of girls who attend school?

A Typical School Day

Activity: Visit **www.citizenkidcentral.com** to print out "A Typical School Day" worksheets. Ask students to fill in their schedule of activities on the left-hand side of the grid. Once they have finished, ask a couple of students to share with the class how their lives are different from those of the girls in Razia's school.

Compare and Contrast:
- chores before and after school
- travel to and from school — length of time and mode of transportation
- who prepares dinner
- electricity supply, and how that affects studying and bedtime

Necessities versus Extras

Activity: Ask students to write down a list of items and activities they spend money on. These should be things that are nice to have, but not necessary (for example, designer clothing, posters, concert tickets, MP3 players, music downloads, fast food, movies and candy, popcorn and drinks). Then have them tally up the annual amount they spend on these extras. After they have done so, share with them the approximate donation needed to educate a girl for one year at Razia's school in Afghanistan.

Annual expenses for a student at Razia's school	Cost ($)
Tuition (pays for building maintenance, teachers' salaries, books, etc.)	200
Uniform (two uniforms, shoes and headscarf)	50
Pencils	1
Notebooks	2
	253

QUESTIONS FOR DISCUSSION:
- In one year, how does the cost of your "extras" compare to the cost of Razia's education?
- What items and activities can you think of that are "nice to have" that cost about the same as a year of school in a developing country?
- How can you use this information to help young people around the world receive an education? Some food for thought: You and your friends might save or raise money to donate by volunteering your time, skills and talents (for example, babysitting, raking leaves, organizing bake sales). Or perhaps you could spread the word on the issue of illiteracy and importance of education (for example, writing articles in the school paper or your house of worship newsletter).

These activities have been adapted and used with permission from the Razia's Ray of Hope Foundation, **www.raziasrayofhope.org**.